IT'S TIME FOR YOUR SCHOOL TO BE BILINGUAL

Here's How

YAIR HERRERA F.

UrbanPress
PUBLISHING YOUR DREAMS

It's Time For Your School To Be Bilingual
by Yair Herrera F

ISBN 978-1-63360-356-1

For Worldwide Distribution Printed in the U.S.A.

Urban Press
PO Box 5044
Williamsburg, VA 23188
757.808.5776
www.urbanpress.us

Contents

chapter 1
About Me 1

chapter 2
Strategic Advantages of a Bilingual Program 6

chapter 3
Pedagogical Model and Methodological Framework for Your Program 12

chapter 4
A Faith-Driven Framework for Bilingual Education 21

chapter 5
Educational Theories and Pedagogical Models in Bilingual Learning 27

chapter 6
Teaching Methodologies in Bilingual Education — From Grammar to CLIL and Beyond 34

chapter 7
Psychological and Sociocultural Foundations of Language Learning 42

chapter 8
Identifying Your School's Current Level of Bilingual Development 49

chapter 9
Choosing the Appropriate English Program for Your School 55

chapter 10
Designing Your Bilingual Curriculum 62

chapter 11
What Does a Language Arts Lesson Look Like in an ESL/EFL Context? 69

chapter 12
Evaluating Progress and Ensuring Accountability 76

chapter 13
Choosing and Training Your Faculty 83

chapter 14
Curriculum Development —
What Should We Teach and When? 89

chapter 15
Engaging Parents and the Community in
Your Bilingual Program 97

Chapter 16
Launching Your Bilingual Program —
The First 90 Days 103

Chapter 17
Be Patient — Bilingualism Takes Time 110

chapter 18
Moving Forward With Purpose —
Your Bilingual Journey Begins 117

chapter 1

About Me

I hadn't originally planned to write this chapter. I told myself the book would stay short and practical. But my editor, Dr. John Stanko, convinced me that before we explore educational models and strategies, you should know where I come from and how Christ has shaped my journey. What you'll read here is not just biography—it's a testimony. My story shows that God can take anyone from chaos to purpose and from fear to faith.

Colombia is divided into neighborhoods by socioeconomic levels, from 0 to 6—level 0 being the poorest. I started life in level 1, in a municipality called Soledad, near Barranquilla. My father wanted my mother to abort me—but God had other plans. Violence filled our home until one day my mother poured boiling water on him and ran away with me when I was four years old. From that point, life became even harder.

I have few memories from those early years. What I do remember are moments of confusion and rejection. When I was ten, I saw my father again at school and ran away because I didn't recognize him. I became overweight and was bullied at school and in my neighborhood. The constant humiliation made me feel worthless, and I often wondered why I was alive.

By the time I was thirteen, I had stopped eating almost entirely—my unhealthy attempt to escape pain. I survived on a piece of bread and a soda each day until I became seriously ill with hepatitis, kidney failure, and other complications. When I finally returned to school, I had lost so much weight that no one recognized me. I had also fallen behind academically, failing several subjects—including English. Yes, I failed English! That irony still makes me smile.

My teacher told me to memorize a list of one hundred words with their Spanish translations. Something unexpected happened—I began to enjoy reading the dictionary's phonetic transcriptions and repeating the sounds. This was 1994, long before Google Translate or AI. Cassette tapes and vinyl records were expensive (look them up if you're under thirty-eight, haha). I studied those words and passed the test.

The following year, my teacher asked a question in class, and I was the only student who understood and answered correctly. That small success changed my life. It awakened something inside me: the realization that I was good at something, that I could learn, teach, and help others. That day, I discovered one expression of my purpose—to equip and show people a better way to live through education and Christ, bringing order out of chaos.

Even with that discovery, my road was not smooth. My parents often told me I was useless and refused to invest in my education. I knew I needed a job. I enrolled in a three-year English course at Universidad del Atlántico in my hometown, and language learning came naturally. Yet I struggled to find work until 2001, when I was accepted as an intern at the Meyer Institute in Barranquilla. I trained for two months without pay before teaching my first class. I was nervous and unprepared. Some lessons were disasters—but every mistake became a lesson in humility and perseverance.

Later that year, I enrolled in a business program at the university and even ranked first in my class. But fear still controlled me. I dropped out not once or twice but seven times. English, however, stayed with me. Teaching English became my anchor and my passion.

I thought money and success would fill the emptiness I carried, but they never did. What truly gave meaning to my life was seeing others grow. I focused my career on the best English institutions in my city—Colombo Americano, Universidad del Atlántico, ITSA Soledad, and Colegio Americano. It was at Colegio Americano that I began teaching in schools and met my extraordinary wife, Carolina.

During that season, God spoke clearly: education was not just a profession—it was my ministry. I completed a degree in *Licenciatura en Lengua Castellana y Comunicaciones* (you can laugh; it wasn't my first choice, but it was what God provided at the time). Ironically, I only taught Critical Reading once—but I learned to read life differently.

After facing financial hardship, Carolina and I left Colegio Americano and moved in with my mother-in-law until we recovered. In 2012, I began a new chapter at Boston International School. What started as a teaching position became a divine assignment. I was asked to help strengthen the English program, and over time, I learned that leadership is not about titles but about service, faith, and learning from others.

At Boston International School, I have had the privilege of witnessing what God can do through vision and teamwork. Some of our milestones include:

- Students certified by A2 Flyers in fifth grade
- B2 certification by the Preliminary English Test in ninth grade
- C1 or C2 certification in eleventh grade through IELTS Academic
- Recognition as a National Bilingual School by the Colombian Government
- Co-founding Best Academy, certified as a TDAH technical institute for education
- Establishing the BIS Foundation to expand opportunities for more students
- Improving curriculum to meet international standards such as the Common Core, CEFR, critical thinking, lifelong learning, and faith integration
- Achieving #1 English school ranking in Colombia in 2024 (ICFES) among more than 7,000 schools

- Serving as external review team leader and evaluator for ICAA with Oral Roberts University and Cognia
- Training and mentoring over thirty teachers annually and speaking at national education events

During this time, I also earned my Master's in Christian Global Leadership from Southwestern Christian University, thanks to a scholarship made possible by Boston International School, Dr. Reggies Wenyika, and Coach Mark Arthur. I am the result of God's work in me, along with the decisions and people He has brought my way. I am especially grateful to the Boston International Schools Network board which has been kind to me, especially Mrs. Ingrid Reyes whose motherly approach and love for Christ have impacted me deeply and Mrs. Luz Danis "Kika" Reyes, whose stewardship and adamant love for God have been a great example of what we can accomplish in Christ.

Outside of school, my life expanded beyond the classroom. I became a more skilled interpreter and now serve Dr. John Stanko as his interpreter and liaison for Latin America. I count him not only as a mentor but as a dear friend. I contributed two chapters to *Strictly Business* (available on Amazon) and later authored what you are now reading, *It's Time For Your School To Be Bilingual.* My dream is for this project to grow into a podcast and YouTube series accessible to every teacher and leader who desires to transform their school through simple, practical, and faith-filled steps.

None of this came easily. Carolina and I married in 2011 and waited years for the gift of children. In time, God answered our prayers with Noah and Nicolas, and He also blessed us with our niece, Simona, who fills our lives with laughter. My marriage is strong, though imperfect. And yes, to all husbands reading this—changing diapers isn't helping; it's your job! (I learned that one the hard way.)

As I write these words, I sense new seasons ahead as I have been appointed the Vice Principal of Boston Flex School. Change is coming again, but I'm not afraid. Every chapter of my life has taught me that when Christ is first, order replaces chaos. My purpose remains clear: *to equip and show people a better way to live through education and Christ, bringing order out of chaos.*

That purpose is not mine alone—it's a call to every believer who teaches, leads, or serves. Education is ministry. Teaching is discipleship. And bilingual education, done with excellence and faith, can transform nations. That is where my story leads—and where yours can begin.

chapter 2

Strategic Advantages of a Bilingual Program

For Our School

I reside in Colombia, a country in South America. Our Ministry of Education provides clear guidelines for the certification of bilingual programs. Two key documents define these standards:

- Guía No. 4 – Manual de evaluación y clasificación de establecimientos educativos privados

- Orientaciones para el fortalecimiento del bilingüismo en instituciones educativas

Once your school complies with these protocols and achieves bilingual certification, the benefits extend far beyond the label of *bilingual*. They influence your school's reputation, culture, and impact on the community.

1. Institutional Recognition

A certified bilingual program earns your school formal recognition from the Colombian government and international accrediting bodies. This demonstrates academic excellence, quality assurance, and alignment with national and international education standards. Parents perceive certified schools as more trustworthy, competitive, and future-oriented. The certification also increases visibility in rankings, attracting new students, and strengthening the institution's financial sustainability.

2. Enhanced Academic Reputation

Bilingual certification communicates that your school prepares students for a globalized world. Universities, employers, and international organizations look for students who are not only fluent in another language but also possess cultural intelligence and adaptability. When a school demonstrates results—such as strong ICFES scores, standardized test success, or IELTS certifications—it becomes a reference point in the community.

3. Staff Development and Teacher Excellence

To reach bilingual status, schools must invest in teacher development. This includes training in communicative methods, English proficiency, classroom observation, and evaluation systems. Teachers grow professionally and spiritually, which directly benefits students. A bilingual school becomes a hub of continuous learning, where teachers learn from one another and pursue excellence together.

4. Global Partnerships

Accredited bilingual institutions often attract partnerships with universities and organizations abroad. Through these alliances, schools can exchange best practices, invite international speakers, and open scholarship opportunities for students. Programs such as ACSI, ICAA, DBU Global Community and Cognia recognize and reward schools that uphold these standards, making global collaboration a natural outcome of faithful stewardship and academic integrity.

5. Community and Mission Impact

For Christian schools, bilingualism is more than an academic advantage—it is a ministry opportunity. English becomes a bridge for evangelism, missions, and intercultural communication. Teachers and students can share God's Word across borders and participate in projects that extend the Kingdom. Excellence in education testifies to the excellence of the God we serve.

For Our Students

A bilingual program multiplies opportunities for students. The most obvious benefit is learning a second language, but the transformation runs deeper—it reshapes how students think, communicate, and relate to the world.

1. Cognitive Growth

Learning in two languages enhances brain flexibility, creativity, and problem-solving skills. Bilingual students tend to develop greater focus, multitasking ability, and memory retention. They learn to approach challenges from multiple perspectives, a crucial skill in today's complex world.

2. Academic Advantage

Students who study in bilingual environments usually perform better in other subjects because language learning improves comprehension, reading, and analytical ability. Exposure to multiple languages strengthens critical thinking and allows them to understand concepts at deeper levels.

3. Cultural Awareness

Through English, students discover new cultures and worldviews, which helps them appreciate diversity. They learn to respect differences and interact gracefully with people from various backgrounds—an essential trait for leadership in a global society.

4. Career Opportunities

English proficiency is a powerful tool for employability. Many multinational companies and universities require it. A bilingual graduate can access scholarships, study abroad, and pursue careers in business, diplomacy, education, and ministry. In a global economy, English is not simply a skill—it is currency.

5. Spiritual Formation

For Christian educators, bilingualism is a spiritual calling. As students read Scripture, worship, and communicate in another language, their understanding of God's world and mission expands. They see how the gospel transcends borders and cultures. This shapes them into global citizens with Kingdom purpose.

Reflection and Purpose

A bilingual program transforms both **school** and **students**. It strengthens institutional excellence while expanding students' vision of the world and God's plan for their lives. However, the true advantage of bilingual education is not in certification or recognition—it is in transformation. When language becomes a tool for serving others, education fulfills its divine purpose.

My hope is that by reading this chapter, you see bilingual education not as an administrative goal but as a Kingdom assignment. As leaders and teachers, we are called to prepare students who can think globally, love deeply, and serve faithfully—*in any language.*

References

Freire, P. (1970). *Pedagogy of the Oppressed*. Herder and Herder.

Gardner, H. (2011). *Frames of Mind: The Theory of Multiple Intelligences*. Basic Books.

Krashen, S. (1982). *Principles and Practice in Second Language Acquisition*. Pergamon Press.

Ministerio de Educación Nacional. *Guía No. 4 – Manual de evaluación y clasificación de establecimientos educativos privados*. https://www.mineducacion.gov.co/portal/micrositios-preescolar-basica-y-media/Educacion-Privada/345218:Guia-No-4-Manual-de-evaluacion-y-clasificacion-de-establecimientos-educativos-privados

Secretaría de Educación de Bogotá. *Orientaciones para el fortalecimiento del bilingüismo en instituciones educativas*. https://www.educacionbogota.edu.co/portal_institucional/sites/default/files/Orientaciones-Bilinguismo.pdf

The Holy Bible, New International Version. (2011). *Matthew 28:19–20; Proverbs 22:6*.

chapter 3

Pedagogical Model and Methodological Framework for Your Program

The whole purpose of this book is to give you practical tools and frameworks to help you turn your school bilingual *now.* This chapter introduces the pedagogical and methodological foundation that supports a strong bilingual education program. Feel free to copy, adapt, or expand any of the material here for your own context. What matters most is that you apply these principles with excellence, purpose, and faith.

1. Pedagogical Foundations

A **pedagogical model** defines *how* students learn, while a **methodological framework** defines *how* teachers teach. In bilingual education, these two must work together to promote communication, comprehension, and cultural understanding. Every school must design its model according to its mission, vision, and values. For Christian institutions, pedagogy must also reflect biblical truth: every learner is created in God's image, gifted with unique talents, and capable of growth through the renewing of the mind (Romans 12:2). Some schools copy foreign models without adapting them to their cultural and spiritual context. That's a mistake. The most effective model is one that integrates theory, faith, and relevance to your community.

2. Key Approaches in Bilingual Education

The following are several well-known methodologies that have proven successful in bilingual and second-language learning environments. Each can be integrated into your school's purpose-driven model.

a. Communicative Language Teaching (CLT)

CLT focuses on helping students *use* language in real-life contexts rather than just memorizing grammar rules. Students engage in conversations, role plays, and problem-solving activities that mirror authentic situations. This approach emphasizes fluency, collaboration, and interaction—key skills for global citizenship.

b. Content and Language Integrated Learning (CLIL)

CLIL combines language learning with subject content. For example, a science class might be taught in English, allowing students to learn both the academic material and the language simultaneously. This approach aligns well with Christian education because it encourages integration—students learn to connect language, knowledge, and purpose.

c. Task-Based Learning (TBL)

Task-Based Learning organizes lessons around meaningful tasks rather than textbook units. Students might design a community project, write a report, or create a presentation—all in English. It builds confidence, teamwork, and autonomy while promoting authentic communication.

d. Constructivism

Based on the theories of Piaget and Vygotsky, constructivism views learners as active participants in building knowledge. Teachers act as facilitators who guide exploration and reflection. A constructivist bilingual classroom promotes inquiry, collaboration, and personal ownership of learning—values consistent with a faith-based vision of stewardship and creativity.

e. Multiple Intelligences Theory

Howard Gardner's theory reminds us that students learn in diverse ways—linguistic, logical, spatial, musical, kinesthetic, interpersonal, intrapersonal, and naturalistic. Bilingual programs that integrate these intelligences become more inclusive, engaging, and effective, reflecting God's creative diversity in His people.

f. Cooperative Learning

In cooperative learning, students work together in small groups to accomplish shared goals. This model builds empathy, leadership, and accountability—skills essential for discipleship and service.

3. Your Curriculum: Integrating Faith and Purpose

A bilingual program rooted in Christian principles must do more than teach English; it must also cultivate *character, calling, and compassion.* Every classroom activity becomes a way to glorify God through excellence, discipline, and collaboration. Teachers model servant leadership, encouraging students to see their bilingual abilities as tools for ministry and global impact. When your school's pedagogy aligns with its faith foundation, education becomes transformational. It equips students not only to succeed academically but to serve meaningfully.

You cannot bring Biblical truth or worldview if your Vision and Mission statements lack them. That's the reason I invite you to revisit them in case you need to make them more visible. Remember what the Apostle Paul wrote: "Do not be ashamed to testify about our Lord" (2 Timothy 1:8).

You want to construct a curriculum that integrates Christian values and principles along with the necessary educational components for effective teaching and learning. Here are some things to keep in mind as you do this.

a. The importance of integrating faith and learning

Integrating faith and academics is essential in Christian education because it:

- Aligns all knowledge with a biblical worldview.
- Develops whole person - spiritually, intellectually, emotionally, and morally.
- Equips students not just for careers, but for **God-honoring lives of service** and purpose.
- Cultivates discernment, wisdom, and a sense of calling in the midst of a secularized world.

"All truth is God's truth." – Arthur F. Holmes (1977)

Faith-learning integration avoids a dualistic view of life where "faith" is restricted to religious activities and "academics" is seen as neutral. Instead, every subject is seen through the lens of **God as Creator**, **Christ as Redeemer**, and the **Bible as the ultimate truth.**

b. Key authors and theorists

The chart that follows shows some influential authors who have shaped the philosophy and practice of faith-integrated education. You will want to explore more of what they have to say.

Author	Contribution
Arthur F. Holmes	Advocated for the integration of Christian worldview into liberal arts education.
Nicholas Wolterstorff	Emphasized justice, shalom, and a Reformed perspective in Christian education.
Harro Van Brummelen	Developed practical frameworks for curriculum design with a biblical worldview.

Author	Contribution
George R. Knight	Wrote extensively on the biblical foundations of Christian education.
David Smith & James K. A. Smith	Promoted a liturgical view of education where pedagogy shapes loves and desires.
John Van Dyk	Focused on a reformed and holistic approach to teaching and curriculum.

4. How to Build a Curriculum Integrating Faith and Academics

a. Start with a biblical worldview

All subjects should be rooted in a framework that recognizes:

- God as the source of all knowledge.
- Humanity's purpose in glorifying God and serving others.
- The redemptive narrative (Creation – Fall – Redemption – Restoration) as the storyline of all learning.

"*A Christian worldview is not just what we believe, but how we see everything.*"
— James Sire (2004)

b. Define Christ-centered educational goals

Goals must go beyond academic excellence. They should develop:

- Spiritual maturity
- Biblical discernment
- Moral and ethical reasoning
- Service-oriented leadership

c. Use faith-integrated learning outcomes

Each subject should include outcomes that:

- Reflect biblical truth.

- Encourage students to see God's hand in the discipline.
- Foster a sense of stewardship and purpose.

For example:

- In **science**, marvel at creation and respect for life.
- In **history**, understand human fallenness and God's providence.
- In **language arts**, develop empathy and ethical communication.

d. Design units around biblical themes

Develop thematic units or essential questions guided by scripture.

- Examples: **justice, stewardship, truth, wisdom, identity in Christ**.

e. Model integration in teacher practices

Teachers are not just conveyors of information but **living curriculum** (Palmer, 2007). Their worldview, relationships, and classroom culture model Christ-likeness.

f. Incorporate spiritual practices

Faith is nurtured through:

- Prayer
- Devotions
- Reflection
- Service-learning
- Worship integrated into the school week and classroom rhythms

g. Engage families and the community

Partnership with Christian families and churches strengthens integration and relevance.

Sample Curriculum Integration Template

Subject	Biblical Theme	Integration Example
Science	Stewardship	Explore environmental care as obedience to God's creation mandate
Math	Order & Design	Recognize God's character through patterns, logic, and precision
History	Justice	Analyze historical events through the lens of human dignity and sin
Literature	Identity	Discuss themes of purpose, morality, and redemption in texts
Art	Creativity	Express God-given creativity and reflect beauty as image-bearers
Physical Ed.	Discipline	Emphasize respect for the body as a temple of the Holy Spirit

5. Building Your School's Model

To develop your own bilingual framework, consider the following practical steps. Clarify your philosophy of education by writing down what you believe about learning, students, and the role of faith in education. Choose your core methodologies by deciding which of the approaches above best fit your context; you don't need to adopt them all—start small and grow intentionally. Train your teachers through consistent professional development in communicative strategies, classroom English, and Christian worldview integration. Document your model by creating a written framework that guides curriculum design, lesson planning, and assessment. Finally, reflect and adjust by reviewing your program annually to ensure it aligns with both ministry goals and academic outcomes.

Reflection and Purpose

A strong pedagogical model gives structure to your school, but a purpose-driven vision gives it life. Methods without mission become mechanical, but when faith informs your teaching philosophy, every lesson becomes a divine opportunity to shape hearts and minds. God calls us not just to teach languages but to build leaders who can think, speak, and serve with excellence—in any language.

References

Gardner, H. (2011). *Frames of Mind: The Theory of Multiple Intelligences.* Basic Books.

Holmes, A. F. (1977). *The Idea of a Christian College*. Eerdmans.

Knight, G. R. (2006). *Philosophy & Education: An Introduction in Christian Perspective* (4th ed.). Andrews University Press.

Krashen, S. (1982). *Principles and Practice in Second Language Acquisition.* Pergamon Press.

Piaget, J. (1970). *Science of Education and the Psychology of the Child.* Orion Press.

Richards, J. C., & Rodgers, T. S. (2014). *Approaches and Methods in Language Teaching.* Cambridge University Press.

The Holy Bible, New International Version. (2011). *Romans 12:2; Proverbs 22:6.*

Van Brummelen, H. (2009). *Walking with God in the Classroom: Christian Approaches to Learning and Teaching* (3rd ed.). Purposeful Design Publications.

Vygotsky, L. S. (1978). *Mind in Society: The Development of Higher Psychological Processes.* Harvard University Press.

chapter 4

A Faith-Driven Framework for Bilingual Education

"To have another language is to possess a second soul." – Charlemagne

As educators, we are not just shaping minds—we are shaping lives, identities, and futures. When we talk about bilingual education, we are not merely transferring grammar rules, vocabulary lists, or pronunciation patterns. We are helping students expand the way they think, connect, communicate, and understand the world God created.

When I speak to school leaders, I often remind them: **bilingual education is not only an academic decision—it is also a philosophical and spiritual one.** What we believe about God, humanity, culture, and knowledge influences how we teach, what we prioritize, and how we define success.

This is why the starting point for bilingual transformation is not a textbook or methodology—but **a worldview.**

The Role of a Christian Worldview in Bilingual Education

As followers of Christ, we believe every person is created in the image of God, with dignity, potential, creativity, and purpose. Our classrooms should reflect that conviction. Students are not empty containers waiting to be filled; they are developing individuals who deserve an environment where excellence, grace, and truth coexist.

One verse that guides me in this work is:

"Start children off on the way they should go, and even when they are old they will not turn from it." —Proverbs 22:6 (NIV)

This verse reminds us that education is formative—it builds direction, identity, habits, and spiritual grounding. Bilingual education, when guided intentionally, helps form students into global citizens who can communicate with empathy and confidence, while remaining spiritually rooted.

Building a Faith-Integrated Bilingual Curriculum

To build a curriculum that honors both language development and spiritual formation, I encourage schools to reflect on the following guiding questions:

- What kind of student do we hope to graduate?
- What values do we want woven into teaching, relationships, and school culture?
- How will bilingual learning strengthen—not replace—their identity in Christ and their sense of calling?

A bilingual program aligned with Christian identity should aim to develop:

- Strong communication skills in the students' native language and English
- A biblical worldview that shapes decisions and understanding
- Cultural awareness and respect for God's diverse global family
- Courage to lead, create, and serve in a multilingual world
- Critical and reflective thinking—expressed with clarity and kindness

This process takes time. But when we commit to it, the results go beyond competencies—they produce character.

Educational Models and Methodologies: Choosing Wisely

Earlier in the book, we explored methods and pedagogical theory. Now, the question becomes **how do we apply them intentionally?** Over the years, I have observed that many schools adopt teaching methods without asking the most important questions:

- Does this methodology respect the dignity of the learner?
- Does it help students think, not only repeat?
- Does it support academic rigor without losing relational warmth?
- Does it match the goals God has placed in our hearts for education?

There are many methodologies available today—from grammar-based instruction to communicative, constructivist, and task-based models. None are perfect, and none need to stand entirely alone. What matters most is alignment: **your method should support your mission.**

For example:

- A **grammar-translation method** may help students recognize patterns, but it should not replace meaningful communication.
- A **communicative approach** encourages speaking and confidence, but it needs structure.

- **CLIL (Content and Language Integrated Learning)** strengthens academic language and global readiness, but teachers must be prepared and trained.

When schools combine thoughtful methodology with a clear worldview and purpose, the bilingual program gains strength and direction.

21st-Century Priorities: Critical Thinking, Innovation, and Purpose

We live in a world that is constantly changing—technology, culture, communication, and expectations are moving fast. To prepare students for the future, a bilingual program must go beyond vocabulary and grammar. It should help students:

- Ask meaningful questions
- Think critically and creatively
- Collaborate and communicate across cultures
- Use language as a tool for learning—not just a subject to pass
- Lead with compassion, wisdom, and a sense of mission

This is where bilingual instruction becomes transformational—not transactional.

Reflection and Next Step

As you move forward, take a moment to reflect:

How does your current bilingual program reflect your deepest beliefs about God, students, and education?

If something feels misaligned, do not worry—this is the moment to strengthen your foundation. Change does not begin with perfection. It begins with **clarity and conviction**. You do not need to overhaul everything at once. Start with one intentional step:

- A conversation with your team
- A revision of one subject's learning goals
- A new routine where students greet or pray in English
- A shared commitment to teach with purpose—not pressure

Over time, these small choices shape a culture that honors both **excellence** and **faith.**

References

The Holy Bible, New International Version. Proverbs 22:6.

Author's personal training, field experience, and bilingual curriculum development (2010–2025).

chapter 5

Educational Theories and Pedagogical Models in Bilingual Learning

"Education is not the filling of a pail,
but the lighting of a fire."
—William Butler Yeats

As educators, we make decisions every day—sometimes consciously, sometimes instinctively—that shape the learning experience of our students. Yet many of those decisions are rooted in educational theories we are rarely taught to name. When we build a bilingual program without understanding the research and ideas behind learning, we risk teaching without intention. But when we align our methods with sound theory, our decisions become stronger, clearer, and more effective.

One of my goals in writing this book is to help you recognize **why you teach the way you teach**, and how your approach can consciously support the bilingual goals of your school.

Why Theory Matters in Bilingual Education

Educational theories are more than academic references—they are tools to guide lesson planning, curriculum design, teacher expectations, assessment, and student engagement. In bilingual contexts, theory matters even more, because language development is not only cognitive; it is **social, emotional, cultural, and experiential.**

Understanding theory helps us:

- Choose teaching approaches that match our learners' developmental stages
- Support students with diverse abilities and paces of learning
- Design activities that promote real communication, not just memorization
- Balance structure with creativity
- Build a program with long-term academic coherence

A well-designed bilingual program is intentional—not accidental.

Key Educational Theorists and Their Contributions

The following page contains a simplified overview of major theorists often referenced in bilingual education. You will see how each brings a different perspective on learning, motivation, and classroom interaction.

Theorist	Core Idea	Relevance to Bilingual Education
Jean Piaget	Learning develops in stages; children construct knowledge through experience	Helps teachers select age-appropriate content and avoid expecting abstract reasoning before students are developmentally ready
Lev Vygotsky	Learning is social; Zone of Proximal Development (ZPD) and scaffolding	Supports pair/group work, modeling, guided language practice, and peer learning
Jerome Bruner	Spiral curriculum; learning reinforced through repeated exposure with increasing complexity	Ideal for bilingual learning where vocabulary and grammar recur at higher cognitive levels
David Ausubel	Meaningful learning, not memorization; connects new learning to prior knowledge	Encourages teachers to activate background knowledge—especially important for ELLs
Howard Gardner	Multiple intelligences; students learn differently	Encourages varied activities: linguistic, musical, kinesthetic, visual, interpersonal
Paulo Freire	Education should empower students and build identity	Reinforces culture, dignity, and student voice in bilingual environments
Stephen Krashen	Second Language Acquisition model; comprehensible input and affective filter	Supports immersion, natural language exposure, and reading as core components

Each of these thinkers contributes something essential: a way to understand students not just as learners of grammar rules, but as whole individuals capable of reasoning, expression, and identity-building through language.

Pedagogical Approaches Connected to Theory

Many schools adopt teaching practices without realizing they belong to larger frameworks. Here is a simplified map linking theory to classroom philosophy.

Approach	Root Theory	Classroom Expression
Behaviorism	Learning through repetition and reinforcement	Drills, chants, flashcards, structured speaking practice
Constructivism	Learners build meaning through experience	Inquiry tasks, guided discovery, project-based learning
Sociocultural Learning	Learning happens through interaction and language	Group tasks, shared reading, modeling, peer support
Humanism	Learning considers emotional and personal growth	Encouragement, relationship-building, student choice
Cognitivism	Understanding matters more than recall	Concept maps, sequencing, reflection checkpoints

What This Means for Your School

When designing a bilingual curriculum, theory becomes a framework—not a constraint. It gives clarity to decisions such as:

- How much teacher talk vs. student talk should occur
- How to scaffold new vocabulary
- When to introduce abstract language structures
- How to support students emotionally during immersion
- How much repetition is helpful—and when it becomes limiting

A strong theoretical foundation keeps us grounded and prevents the program from shifting with every new trend or textbook.

Putting Theory Into Practice

Below are examples of how theory translates into classroom habits:

- If you value **Vygotsky**, you will plan collaborative learning.
- If you apply **Bruner**, you will revisit language structures in increasing complexity over time.
- If you apply **Gardner**, you will diversify learning modalities and recognize student strengths.
- If you apply **Krashen**, you will focus on meaningful input and reduce performance anxiety.

The best programs do **not** choose one theorist or one model. They create a thoughtful blend that serves real students in real classrooms.

Reflection

As you consider this chapter, ask yourself:

Which theories currently guide your teaching—and which ones do you want to integrate moving forward?

Understanding the "why" behind your teaching makes your program stronger, your decisions clearer, and your students' learning experience more meaningful.

References

Ausubel, D. (1968). *Educational Psychology: A Cognitive View.*

Bruner, J. (1960). *The Process of Education.*

Freire, P. (1970). *Pedagogy of the Oppressed.*

Gardner, H. (1983). *Frames of Mind: The Theory of Multiple Intelligences.*

Krashen, S. (1982). *Principles and Practice in Second Language Acquisition.*

Piaget, J. (1926). *Language and Thought of the Child.*

Vygotsky, L. (1978). *Mind in Society.*

chapter 6

Teaching Methodologies in Bilingual Education — From Grammar to CLIL and Beyond

"Tell me and I forget. Teach me and I remember. Involve me and I learn."
—Benjamin Franklin

When we talk about bilingual education, many people immediately think of textbooks, vocabulary lists, and English-only rules. Yet behind every teaching decision lies a deeper question: **How do students actually learn a new language best?**

Methods in language teaching have evolved over time—not because old ideas were useless, but because our understanding of learning has grown. Each approach emerged from a context, a belief about how the mind learns, and a purpose. Some methods focused on accuracy and structure, while others prioritized communication and confidence.

As leaders building or strengthening a bilingual program, understanding these methodologies helps us make better decisions—not just repeat habits or follow the newest trend.

A Brief Journey Through Language Teaching Approaches

Below is a simplified timeline showing how methodologies evolved and what they emphasized. You will likely recognize pieces of each one in your school today.

Method	Era	Main Focus	Strength	Limitation
Grammar-Translation Method	1800s	Rules, structure, translation	Strong reading/ writing base	Weak speaking fluency
Direct Method	Early 1900s	Learning through immersion and speaking	Real-life communication	Requires skilled teachers
Audio-Lingual Method	1950-1970	Repetition, drills, memorized patterns	Strong pronunciation habits	Limited creative language use
Cognitive-Code Learning	1970s	Understanding rules + meaningful use	Good balance of structure + thinking	Still teacher-centered
Communicative Approach (CLT)	1980s-Present	Meaningful communication and fluency	Student-centered; builds confidence	Grammar sometimes unclear

Method	Era	Main Focus	Strength	Limitation
Task-Based Learning (TBLT)	1990s-Present	Learning through purposeful tasks	Real-world application	Requires planning and scaffolding
Content and Language Integrated Learning (CLIL)	2000s-Present	Teaching subjects through English	Strong bilingual competency	Requires trained teachers and planning

Each methodology brings something valuable. Instead of choosing just one, we build a bilingual program by selecting what supports our goals.

Methodology in Practice: Strengths, Misuses, and Balance

As a bilingual leader, you will notice that teaching styles vary from teacher to teacher. Some naturally teach through structure and precision; others teach through participation and expression.

Neither extreme is ideal on its own.

- A program focused **only on grammar** produces students who pass exams but fear speaking.
- A program focused **only on communication** may produce confident speakers with weak writing or reading discipline.

A healthy bilingual program combines:

- **Accuracy** (grammar, syntax, vocabulary control)
- **Fluency** (confidence, meaning, communication)

This balance does not happen by accident—it happens by design.

Communicative Language Teaching (CLT): Still Relevant, But Not Enough

One of the most influential approaches today is CLT. Many bilingual teachers use it—some intentionally, others because it feels natural.

CLT encourages:

- Pair and group work
- Authentic communication
- Speaking with purpose, not perfection
- Real-world tasks ("order food," "debate," "ask directions")

However, without structure, CLT can drift into "talking without learning." Vocabulary expands, but accuracy may not.

In bilingual schools, this method works best when paired with **intentional grammar instruction and guided feedback.**

Task-Based Learning (TBLT): Language With Purpose

Task-Based Learning builds on CLT by designing learning around meaningful tasks such as:

- Planning a trip
- Solving a problem
- Completing a project
- Presenting research

Students acquire language because they **need it to accomplish a goal.**

This mirrors real life: we learn language when there is a purpose.

CLIL: A Modern Standard in Bilingual Schools

CLIL (Content and Language Integrated Learning) is increasingly recognized as the method of choice for bilingual and international programs.

In CLIL, academic subjects such as:

- Science
- Math
- History
- Art

are taught through the target language—in this case, English.

CLIL promotes:

- Academic vocabulary
- Interdisciplinary thinking
- Real communication
- Higher-order cognitive skills

To succeed, CLIL requires:

- Teacher training
- Clear scaffolding
- Assessment aligned with both content and language objectives

When CLIL is combined with strong reading, grammar support, and speaking routines, it becomes one of the most powerful models for bilingual learning.

STEM and ELT: Preparing Students for a Changing World

A recent development in bilingual education is the integration of **STEM (Science, Technology, Engineering, and Math)** concepts into English learning. This reflects a global shift: employers are seeking individuals who can communicate, think critically, solve problems, and collaborate across languages and cultures.

STEM-integrated ELT supports:

- Inquiry-based learning
- Problem solving
- Collaboration and design thinking

- Creativity with real-world outcomes

Students are not just learning English—they are learning **in English** while applying skills needed for global citizenship.

A Biblical Lens of Excellence

"Christian worldview begins in the heart of the reformed educator who wholeheartedly brings his/her gifts to the service of others."
—Yair Herrera F.

As a follower of Jesus, I believe excellence honors God. Whatever method we choose should reflect intentionality, dignity, and purpose.

One verse that reminds me of this is:

"So whether you eat or drink, or whatever you do, do it all for the glory of God."
—1 Corinthians 10:31

Bilingual education is not just a teaching method—it is a ministry of transformation, identity, and opportunity.

Reflection

Take a quiet moment to consider:

Which methods are currently used in your school, and which ones align best with your mission and your students' needs?

You don't need to adopt everything at once. Start with clarity, then take one intentional step forward.

References

Brown, H. (2001). *Teaching by Principles: An Interactive Approach to Language Pedagogy.*

Coyle, D., Hood, P., & Marsh, D. (2010). *CLIL: Content and Language Integrated Learning.*

Harmer, J. (2007). *The Practice of English Language Teaching.*

Krashen, S. (1982). *Principles and Practice in Second Language Acquisition.*

Richards, J., & Rodgers, T. (2014). *Approaches and Methods in Language Teaching.*

Willis, J. (1996). *A Framework for Task-Based Learning.*

chapter 7

Psychological and Sociocultural Foundations of Language Learning

"We learn a language not only with the mind,
but with the heart."
—Unknown

When students learn a new language, they are not just memorizing words or grammar. They are navigating identity, confidence, culture, memory, motivation, and emotion. In bilingual education, learning happens on multiple levels: cognitive, social, emotional, and spiritual.

Understanding the psychological and sociocultural foundations of language learning helps us support students more compassionately and effectively. It ensures we respond not only to academic needs, but also to the very real internal challenges they face as they grow into bilingual communicators.

The Emotional Side of Learning a New Language

Language learning can feel vulnerable. When students speak in a second language, they may feel younger, less confident, or afraid of making mistakes. This is normal.

Some students:

- Are eager to participate
- Learn quickly
- Experiment with new vocabulary

Others:

- Stay silent
- Fear embarrassment
- Understand more than they express

Both groups are learning — just differently.

Stephen Krashen calls this the **Affective Filter**, explaining that *when anxiety is high, language learning slows; when confidence grows, learning accelerates.*

This means that classroom culture matters as much as curriculum.

BICS and CALP: A Key Concept for Bilingual Schools

One of the most important frameworks for understanding bilingual development comes from Jim Cummins, who distinguishes between:

Term	Meaning	Timeline
BICS	Basic interpersonal communication skills (social language)	6 months to 2 years

Term	Meaning	Timeline
CALP	Cognitive academic language proficiency (academic language)	5 to 7 years

A student who appears fluent in conversation may still struggle with academic reading or writing. Many schools mistakenly assume a child "is bilingual" after acquiring BICS, when in reality they still need support developing CALP.

Recognizing this difference prevents premature conclusions and helps schools plan long-term support.

Motivation and Identity in Bilingual Learning

Motivation is a driving factor in language acquisition. Students learn faster when they have purpose—a reason to speak, read, write, or engage. Three forms of motivation commonly appear in bilingual programs:

- **Instrumental Motivation** – learning for a goal: grades, jobs, certification
- **Integrative Motivation** – learning to connect with culture, identity, community
- **Intrinsic Motivation** – learning because it is interesting or enjoyable

Students flourish when motivation becomes **internal**, not just school-driven.

Language also shapes identity. Some students feel empowered learning English; others may fear losing their home language or culture. Supporting both languages affirms dignity, belonging, and purpose.

Social Interaction and the Power of Community

Lev Vygotsky tells us that learning is social – it happens in interaction, not isolation. The classroom becomes a laboratory where students practice language with peers, teachers, and community. Practical examples:

- Pair work
- Debate and dialogue

- Cooperative tasks
- Peer teaching
- Shared reading
- Group projects

These interactions build **confidence**, not just competence.

In bilingual programs, language becomes a bridge—connecting students to cultures, ideas, and people they may never have encountered otherwise.

The Role of Culture in Language Learning

Pierre Bourdieu introduced the idea of **linguistic capital**—the value society assigns to certain languages. In many countries, English is associated with education, opportunity, and global access. While this can motivate learners, it also introduces tension:

- Will students feel proud of their bilingual identity—or ashamed of their first language?
- Does the program honor both languages equally?
- Are we teaching English *in addition to* culture—or *instead of* culture?

A healthy bilingual program respects and preserves the student's first language and cultural identity while expanding their world through English.

A Christ-Centered Understanding of the Learner

As Christian educators, we believe each learner is uniquely created, with strengths, needs, and potential. A verse that continually guides me is:

"Be devoted to one another in love. Honor one another above yourselves."
—Romans 12:10

This reminds us that bilingual education is not about producing perfect test scores—it is about honoring God's design in every learner and walking with them as they grow.

Supporting Students Through the Psychological Journey

Students thrive when they experience:

- Safety – "I am not afraid to speak."
- Belonging – "My identity matters."
- Encouragement – "Improvement is noticed."
- Purpose – "English connects me to opportunity."

We build these conditions through consistency, clear expectations, patient correction, and meaningful relationships.

Reflection

Take a moment to consider:

How well does your learning environment support the emotional and social needs of bilingual students—not just their academic progress?

A strong bilingual program teaches English – but an excellent one builds confidence, identity, and belonging.

References

Bourdieu, P. (1991). *Language and Symbolic Power.*

Cummins, J. (1979). *Cognitive Academic Language Proficiency and the Achievement Gap.*

Krashen, S. (1982). *Principles and Practice in Second Language Acquisition.*

Vygotsky, L. (1978). *Mind in Society.*

chapter 8

Identifying Your School's Current Level of Bilingual Development

"You can't improve what you don't measure."
– Peter Drucker

Before designing or improving a bilingual program, every school must first understand its current reality. Vision becomes meaningful when paired with reflection, honesty, and data. This chapter will help you determine where your institution stands today and what steps are needed to move forward strategically. In my workshops with school leaders across Latin America, I often begin with a simple question:

> **"What kind of bilingual school do you believe you are – and what kind of bilingual school do you want to become?"**

Sometimes the answer is clear. Other times, leaders discover a gap between what they *hope* the program is and what is actually happening in daily practice. This chapter will guide you through that discovery process.

Start with A Reflection

Before we analyze structures or strategies, take a moment to reflect individually or with your team:

- How did you learn English or another language when you were a student?
- Which teacher made the greatest impact on your learning? Why?
- How do you want your students to remember their bilingual learning experience?

These questions matter because bilingual programs are not just curriculum—they are culture. They influence how students feel, communicate, learn, and see themselves.

Three Levels of Bilingual Identity

Through my experience evaluating schools, I have identified **three general stages of bilingual development.** Schools rarely fit perfectly into one category; rather, they show characteristics of each stage. Still, this framework helps establish a baseline.

Category	Level 1: Beginning EFL Program	Level 2: Developing Bilingual Program	Level 3: Full Bilingual School (ESL Model)
English Exposure	1-3 hours/week	4-6 hours/week	50% or more of subjects in English
Teacher Proficiency	A2-B1	B2-C1	B2-C2

Category	Level 1: Beginning EFL Program	Level 2: Developing Bilingual Program	Level 3: Full Bilingual School (ESL Model)
Cultural Integration	None	Occasional events (Flag Day, Spelling Bee)	Cultural identity is part of curriculum
Parent Program Awareness	Minimal	Mentioned at orientation	Parents trained, informed, engaged
Staff Training	None	Task-based meetings, peer support	Ongoing mentoring and language development
Hiring Standards	Available teachers	Screening for English proficiency	Recruiting bilingual educators and developing future staff
Community and Communication	No English beyond class	Some English in events/materials	English present across programs, social media, and environment
Academic Alignment	National standards only	Standards with English support	National + international standards

Use this table not to judge, but to understand where your school currently lives — and what steps will build maturity.

Checklist: What Will Your Curriculum Include?

Select the elements you already have and those you want to implement next:

- English as a Second Language (ESL) model
- Content taught in English (CLIL)
- Cultural studies and awareness
- International certification pathway
- Reading plan (graded readers + authentic texts)

- Summer immersion experiences
- Technology and AI integration
- Debate / MUN / public speaking
- Teacher certification pathway
- English literacy benchmarks by grade
- Rubrics and feedback systems
- Extracurricular supports (clubs, camps, tutoring)

No program should attempt everything at once. Instead, choose what aligns with your mission and timeline.

Improvement Pathway: Four Steps Forward

Growing a bilingual program is a process. I describe it in four stages:

1. Identity — Define Who You Are
What does bilingualism mean in your school culture?

2. Assessment — Understand Where You Stand
Use data, interviews, and observation–not assumptions.

3. Alignment — Connect Vision to Practice
Adjust curriculum, teaching expectations, and leadership language.

4. Implementation — Take the Next Right Step
Change begins with small, consistent decisions.

A Simple Exercise for Your Leadership Team

Ask each leader to independently answer:

"Which level do you believe our school is operating in today — Level 1, Level 2, or Level 3?"

Then compare responses. The discussion that follows will reveal valuable insights about alignment, communication, reality, and expectations.

A Word of Encouragement

Do not rush the process. Growth requires patience, consistency, and unity. As Scripture reminds us:

> *"Let us not become weary in doing good, for at the proper time we will reap a harvest if we do not give up."*–Galatians 6:9

Your school's bilingual journey is not just administrative–it is transformative.

References

Author field experience and institutional bilingual assessments (2012–2025).

Coyle, D., Hood, P., & Marsh, D. (2010). *CLIL: Content and Language Integrated Learning.*

Ministry of Education Colombia (Bilingualism Guidelines, 2025).

chapter 9

Choosing the Appropriate English Program for Your School

"The best decisions are made when vision and reality walk together."
—Anonymous

Before building or improving a bilingual program, every school must make one foundational decision:

What kind of English program aligns with who we are and who we want to become?

Many institutions jump into bilingual education because the idea feels exciting, competitive, or modern. But without alignment to identity, purpose, and long-term strategy, the process becomes stressful, expensive, and inconsistent. Schools may change textbooks repeatedly, hire teachers without a framework to support them, or shift expectations from year to year.

Choosing the appropriate English model is not just an academic decision – it is a strategic leadership decision.

Understanding the Purpose Behind Your English Program

Before selecting a program structure, pause and ask:

- Why do we want to strengthen English learning?
- Is our motivation academic, cultural, global, spiritual—or all of these?
- What opportunities do we want to open for our students?

Some schools want students to:

- Communicate confidently
- Succeed in standardized exams
- Access international universities
- Engage with global culture
- Strengthen leadership and mission opportunities

Your answer will guide the model you choose.

Types of English Programs

Most schools fall into one of the following models. Each has strengths – and responsibilities.

Model	Description	Strengths	Considerations
EFL (English as a Foreign Language)	English taught like any other subject	Simple to implement	Limited exposure and fluency
ESL (English as a Second Language)	English used for communication and support across subjects	Builds proficiency and confidence	Requires trained teachers and structure
Bilingual (Partial Immersion)	Some content areas taught in English	Strong academic vocabulary	Requires long-term planning and standards
Full Bilingual / Immersion	50% or more instruction in English	Highest mastery and certification potential	Requires systemic change and professional development

There is no "best" model–the best model is the one that aligns with your capacity, vision, and philosophy.

Key Considerations Before Choosing a Model

When selecting the right path, evaluate the following:

1. Teacher capacity

- What is the current English proficiency of the teaching staff?
- Are there support structures for coaching, mentoring, or certification?

Without teacher development, program goals remain theoretical.

2. Student needs and context

Students do not all learn English for the same purpose. Understanding your school community helps determine the model. Examples:

- A missionary school may prioritize global ministry skills.

- A STEM-focused school may emphasize English for research and innovation.

3. Curriculum and assessment requirements

Some questions to ask:

- Will you align to **national standards only**, or also to **international frameworks** such as CEFR, Cambridge, TOEFL, or IELTS?
- Will the school pursue recognition as a **test preparation center** or **exam partner**?

Certifications provide credibility—but require planning.

4. Institutional identity and values

Your bilingual program should reflect your culture—not replace it. For Christian schools, bilingual education becomes an opportunity to prepare students to serve globally with confidence, excellence, and humility.

Avoiding Common Mistakes When Selecting a Program

Here are frequent pitfalls I have seen in schools across Latin America:

- Choosing books before choosing vision
- Expecting fast results without long-term planning
- Ignoring teacher training and support
- Changing methodology every year
- Believing bilingualism is only about hours rather than strategy

Growth requires patience and alignment—not shortcuts.

A Simple Decision Framework

Use this process with your leadership team:

1. Clarify your purpose.
2. Select the program model that supports that purpose.
3. Ensure alignment with curriculum, staff development, and standards.

4. Communicate the decision clearly to teachers and parents.

Consistency builds trust – and trust strengthens implementation.

A Verse for Guidance

As leaders, we are called to steward decisions wisely:

"Commit to the Lord whatever you do, and He will establish your plans."
—Proverbs 16:3

Choosing a program is not only administrative—it is vision stewardship.

Reflection

Which program model best aligns with your school's identity and long-term mission—and what first step can you take to evaluate readiness?

Take time to discuss, reflect, and listen to your team. Clarity today prevents confusion tomorrow.

References

Author field experience and bilingual school assessments (2012–2025).

Coyle, D., Hood, P., & Marsh, D. (2010). *CLIL: Content and Language Integrated Learning.*

Harmer, J. (2007). *The Practice of English Language Teaching.*

Richards, J., & Rodgers, T. (2014). *Approaches and Methods in Language Teaching.*

chapter 10

Designing Your Bilingual Curriculum

"A goal without a plan is only a wish."
—Antoine de Saint-Exupéry

Once your school has selected the bilingual model that aligns with its identity and mission, the next step is to design a curriculum that supports that choice. A strong bilingual curriculum is intentional—not borrowed, not improvised, and not the result of simply purchasing textbooks.

Curriculum design requires reflection, planning, alignment, and patience. When done well, it becomes the roadmap that shapes instruction, supports teachers, guides assessment, and helps students grow confidently in both language and content.

Start with the End in Mind

Before choosing materials or scheduling class hours, ask yourself:

- What should a student graduating from our school be able to do in English?
- What level of the CEFR or other framework will we use as our benchmark?
- How will we measure progress along the way?

A clear destination prevents frustration and inconsistency.

Examples of measurable end goals:

- Students in Grade 5 reach **A2**
- Students in Grade 9 reach **B1**
- Students graduate at **B2-C1**, prepared for certifications such as Cambridge, TOEFL, or IELTS

When the goal is clear, everything else becomes easier to design.

A strong bilingual curriculum includes the following elements:

- Skill development (listening, speaking, reading, writing)
- Academic vocabulary
- Grammar and structures
- Content-area language demands
- Culture and global competence
- Assessment and certification alignment
- Clear yearly progression goals

Curriculum is more than "what we teach." It is **why, how, and in what order we teach it.**

Selecting Instructional Resources

Resources can support your curriculum—but they cannot replace it. Consider:

- Textbooks and digital platforms
- Graded and authentic readers
- Speaking and listening tools
- Assessment resources
- Teacher training materials

Choose resources **after** defining your program—not before.

Content and Language Integrated Learning (CLIL) Approach

If your school selected a bilingual or immersion model, consider integrating subject instruction in English. This may include:

- Science
- Mathematics
- History
- Art
- Technology

CLIL strengthens both English proficiency and academic understanding by making language the vehicle—not merely the subject.

Key principles of CLIL are:

- Language is learned through meaning and context
- Students receive scaffolding and support
- Teachers collaborate across departments

A CLIL curriculum is best implemented gradually, starting with one or two subjects.

Teacher Expectations and Classroom Practices

A curriculum cannot succeed without alignment in the classroom. Clear expectations help teachers work confidently and consistently.

Some examples:

- English used as the primary classroom language
- Visual supports and scaffolding
- Regular speaking routines
- Assessment rubrics aligned to the model
- Collaboration between Spanish and English faculty

Provide coaching—not pressure. A curriculum is a living document, not a rigid rulebook.

Assessment and Growth Tracking

Assessment should measure **progress**, not just performance. Use a combination of:

- Formative assessments (ongoing checks)
- Summative assessments (unit evaluations)
- Speaking assessments
- Writing portfolios
- External certification benchmarks

Assessment tells the story of growth—and guides instructional decisions.

Curriculum Components to Consider

Start Small, Grow Consistently

Many schools feel overwhelmed by curriculum design because they try to change everything at once. Instead, begin with one grade level, one subject, or one framework—then expand. Small steps taken consistently build strong systems.

A Biblical Reminder in the Process

Curriculum work requires patience and perseverance. This verse encourages me when the process feels slow:

"Whatever you do, work at it with all your heart, as working for the Lord."
–Colossians 3:23

Your curriculum is more than academic planning–it is an act of stewardship for the futures entrusted to your school.

Reflection

Which part of your curriculum is strongest — and which part needs the most intentional development?

Discuss this with your leadership or teaching team and agree on **one first improvement step**.

References

Coyle, D., Hood, P., & Marsh, D. (2010). *CLIL: Content and Language Integrated Learning.*

Harmer, J. (2007). *The Practice of English Language Teaching.*

Richards, J., & Rodgers, T. (2014). *Approaches and Methods in Language Teaching.*

Author field experience and bilingual school implementation plans (2012–2025).

chapter 11

What Does a Language Arts Lesson Look Like in an ESL/EFL Context?

"Great teaching is not just delivering information–it is creating transformation."
–Unknown

Once a bilingual program is chosen and the curriculum is set in motion, the next practical question arises:

"What should an English lesson look like in our classrooms?"

Schools may have the right books, a clear model, and motivated teachers—but without consistent instructional patterns, the experience becomes uneven. Some teachers lean on grammar only, others focus on conversation, and others rely heavily on worksheets.

A successful bilingual program requires **structure with flexibility, intentionality with personality, and consistency with creativity.** This chapter will help define the essential elements of a strong Language Arts lesson in both **ESL (English as a Second Language)** and **EFL (English as a Foreign Language)** environments.

A Lesson With Purpose

A strong English lesson is more than exposure to vocabulary or activities—it is a purposeful learning experience that supports:

- Communication
- Confidence
- Accuracy
- Fluency
- Growth in all four core skills:

Listening, Speaking, Reading, and Writing

The goal is not perfection, but **progress.** Even small, meaningful steps—taken over time—create lasting bilingual competence.

Core Characteristics of an Effective English Lesson

Whether the model is EFL, ESL, bilingual, or partial immersion, strong Language Arts instruction typically includes:

- A clear objective aligned to curriculum goals
- Balanced skill development
- Opportunities for meaningful student speaking
- Feedback that guides improvement

- Interactive learning, not just passive listening
- Exposure to authentic or semi-authentic English
- Celebration of effort—not only correctness

When these elements work together, the classroom becomes a place where students are not afraid to try, fail, learn, and grow.

A Practical Lesson Structure

The following template provides a flexible but consistent structure schools can apply across grade levels. It is not meant to limit creativity; rather, it ensures that every lesson includes essential learning moments.

Stage	Component	Purpose
1	**Warm-Up (Activation)**	Connect with prior knowledge and stimulate language
2	**Explicit Instruction (Mini-Lesson)**	Introduce the lesson focus clearly and simply
3	**Guided Practice**	Model language and support students as they practice
4	**Independent or Group Work**	Allow students to apply learning meaningfully
5	**Speaking or Output Moment**	Ensure students use the language—not only hear it
6	**Reflection or Exit Ticket**	Assess understanding and close the learning cycle

Example Lesson Flow (30–50 Minutes)

1. Greeting and English routine (2-3 min)

- Prayer if appropriate
- English classroom expressions (consistent routine)

2. Warm-up or Review Activity (5 min)

- Song, flashcards, retrieval practice, short speaking routine

3. Mini-Lesson (7-10 min)

- Short, focused teaching: structure, vocabulary, skill strategy

4. Guided Practice (5-8 min)

- Teacher models → students imitate → controlled interaction

5. Independent or Group Application (8-15 min)

- Project, writing task, reading task, partner work, real-life scenario

6. Speaking Output Moment (2-5 min)

- A structured opportunity to speak: role-play, response sentence, think-pair-share

7. Closing + Formative Check (2-3 min)

- Exit ticket, short reflection, self-assessment, or quick teacher feedback

Feedback: The Secret Ingredient

Feedback is most powerful when it is:

- Immediate
- Gentle
- Clear
- Actionable
- Encouraging

Instead of:

❌ *"No, that is wrong."*

Try:

✔ *"Good try. Let's say it again using the correct past tense."*

Students grow when correction feels like support—not failure.

Faith, Identity, and Confidence

If your school integrates Christian values, remember:

Every student carries dignity because God created them in His image—and that includes their learning journey.

A simple verse that reminds us of this is:

"The wise in heart are called discerning, and gracious words promote instruction."
—Proverbs 16:21

Language learning thrives in classrooms where grace and excellence walk together.

A Classroom Checklist for Teachers

Question	Yes	Not Yet
Did I speak mostly in English during instruction?	☐	☐
Did students have multiple opportunities to speak English?	☐	☐
Did the lesson include listening, reading, writing, and speaking elements?	☐	☐
Was feedback clear, kind, and helpful?	☐	☐
Did every student participate—not only the confident ones?	☐	☐
Did the lesson connect to the curriculum goal?	☐	☐

Progress begins with awareness.

Reflection

What part of your English lessons already reflects strong bilingual teaching—and what one element will you intentionally strengthen next week?

Even one consistent change can transform instruction over time.

References

Coyle, D., Hood, P., & Marsh, D. (2010). *CLIL: Content and Language Integrated Learning.*

Harmer, J. (2007). *The Practice of English Language Teaching.*

Scrivener, J. (2010). *Teaching English: A Practical Guide.*

Author classroom leadership experience in bilingual schools (2012–2025).

chapter 12

Evaluating Progress and Ensuring Accountability

"If you can't measure it, you can't manage it."— W. Edwards Deming

A bilingual program does not grow by enthusiasm alone. It grows through reflection, evaluation, and intentional follow-through. Once you establish a curriculum and instructional model, the next essential step is to create systems that help you track progress—not only for your students, but also for teachers, leadership, and the school as a whole.

Evaluation is not about pressure. It is about clarity, growth, and shared purpose. When we measure progress wisely and consistently, we honor the investment of time, training, and prayer that has gone into building the program.

Why Evaluation Matters

In bilingual education, growth can be slow and sometimes invisible in the early stages. Students may understand far more than they are able to express. Teachers may feel unsure whether their methods are working. Parents may question whether the bilingual program is worth the effort.

Meaningful evaluation:

- Builds confidence
- Strengthens communication
- Aligns everyone around shared goals
- Guides next steps
- Protects the long-term vision

A well-designed evaluation system helps everyone see the journey—not only the destination.

Three Areas That Must Be Evaluated

Effective bilingual evaluation considers three dimensions:

1. Student growth

This includes:

- English proficiency benchmarks
- Reading levels
- Speaking confidence
- Listening comprehension
- Writing ability
- Certification readiness

A combination of formal and informal tools creates a complete picture.

2. Instructional quality

We must evaluate:

- Lesson planning
- Classroom routines
- Teacher English proficiency
- Student engagement
- Use of academic language
- Consistency with the school's methodology

Evaluation should be supportive—not intimidating.

3. Program integrity

This category asks:

- Are we still aligned with our vision?
- Are we applying our methodology consistently?
- Are we improving from year to year?
- Do teachers, parents, and students understand the program?

Vision must guide execution—not the other way around.

Tools for Measuring Student Progress

Use a combination of:

- Speaking checklists
- Reading fluency indicators
- Writing rubrics
- Listening comprehension activities
- Vocabulary tracking charts
- Portfolio collections

- Benchmark exams and external certifications

Remember: fluency develops differently for each student. Progress—even slow progress—is success.

Teacher Reflection and Accountability

A healthy bilingual program requires ongoing teacher development and reflection. Instead of relying only on formal observations, encourage teachers to participate in:

- Peer observations
- Lesson study cycles
- Professional learning communities
- English fluency improvement goals
- Self-evaluation rubrics

Accountability becomes healthy when it feels like encouragement, not judgment.

Communicating Progress with Parents

Parents are essential partners in bilingual education. They do better when they understand:

- What their child can do
- What the next step will be
- How they can support learning at home

Practical tools include:

- Parent workshops
- Progress dashboards
- Quarterly feedback reports
- Celebration days
- Student presentations or performances

When families understand the process, motivation increases.

Celebration and Recognition

Progress should not only be measured—it should be celebrated. Celebrate:

- Certification milestones
- Improved confidence
- Effort and perseverance
- Teachers who demonstrate innovation
- Students who encourage others

Celebration builds momentum and strengthens school culture.

A Scriptural Perspective

Evaluation is part of stewardship. Scripture reminds us:

"Let each one examine his own work."—Galatians 6:4a (NKJV)

Evaluation is not about comparison—it is about growth, responsibility, and excellence.

Reflection

How do you currently measure progress in your bilingual program—and where could your evaluation become clearer, more consistent, or more purposeful?

Take time with your leadership and teaching teams to agree on one new evaluation action you will implement in the coming term.

References

Brown, H. (2001). *Teaching by Principles: An Interactive Approach to Language Pedagogy.*
Cambridge English Assessment Frameworks.
Coyle, D., Hood, P., & Marsh, D. (2010). *CLIL: Content and Language Integrated Learning.*
Author field observation and bilingual school evaluation models (2013–2025).

chapter 13

Choosing and Training Your Faculty

"A bilingual program is only as strong as the people who carry it."
—Yair Herrera F.

No matter how strong your curriculum, resources, or vision may be, the heart of your bilingual program is your faculty. Teachers bring the plan to life—one lesson, one interaction, one encouragement at a time.

Choosing the right faculty and equipping them with consistent support is one of the most impactful decisions your school will make. This chapter will guide you through selecting, developing, and nurturing educators who will build and sustain your bilingual vision.

What Makes a Great Bilingual Teacher?

Contrary to popular belief, the best bilingual teachers are not simply those with the highest English proficiency. While language mastery matters, it is only part of the picture. The qualities that matter most include:

- A teachable heart
- A growth mindset
- Cultural humility
- Love for students
- Consistency and professionalism
- Alignment with the mission of the school

A high English level without character quickly becomes a barrier. A teacher with passion and willingness to grow can be shaped into an anchor for your bilingual program.

Teacher Profile Standards

When hiring or evaluating bilingual faculty, consider developing expectations such as:

Category	Beginning	Developing	Proficient
English Level	A2-B1	B2	C1-C2
Training	Basic ELT/ESL awareness	Some methodology training	Complete methodological alignment
Instruction	Teacher-centered	Blended approaches	Student-centered and communicative

Category	Beginning	Developing	Proficient
Collaboration	Rarely collaborates	Willing with support	Actively seeks teamwork and growth
Vision Alignment	Uncertain	Learning process	Fully embraces the bilingual mission

This framework provides clarity not only for leaders but also for teachers themselves.

Training Your Faculty

Teacher development is not a one-time workshop—it is a process.

Strong bilingual programs invest in:

- Internal coaching
- Mentoring systems
- Professional development pathways
- Language improvement opportunities
- Spiritual formation (for faith-based schools)

Teachers grow when they feel supported and challenged at the same time.

A Suggested Training Plan

Area	Focus	Frequency
Language Proficiency	English fluency, academic language	Weekly or biweekly
Methodology	CLT, TBLT, CLIL, teaching strategies	Monthly
Curriculum	Lesson planning, standards alignment	Every 6-8 weeks
Coaching	Classroom observation + feedback	Once per term

Area	Focus	Frequency
Faith and Calling (optional)	Biblical worldview, mission alignment	Quarterly

Building a Culture of Excellence

A healthy team environment encourages:

- Collaboration over competition
- Improvement over perfection
- Reflection over rigid compliance

Encourage teachers to:

- Observe each other
- Share resources
- Celebrate progress
- Ask for help without fear

When teachers feel safe, students benefit.

Retaining Your Teachers

A common challenge in bilingual programs is staff turnover. Teachers often leave not because of salary alone, but because they lack:

- Growth opportunities
- Purpose
- Support
- Clear expectations
- Community

Retention improves when schools communicate:

- Vision

- Encouragement
- Trust

Investing in your faculty is one of the most strategic financial decisions you can make.

A Word of Spiritual Encouragement

For Christian educators, developing others is not only academic—it is discipleship.

"And He gave... teachers, to equip His people for works of service."
—Ephesians 4:11-12

You are not just hiring teachers—you are appointing mentors who will shape generations.

Reflection

Which areas of your current faculty development are strong—and which require intentional improvement to support your bilingual vision?

Discuss this with your leadership team and commit to one clear next action.

References

Coyle, D., Hood, P., & Marsh, D. (2010). *CLIL: Content and Language Integrated Learning.*

Richards, J., & Rodgers, T. (2014). *Approaches and Methods in Language Teaching.*

TESOL International Association Standards for Developing Teachers.

Author coaching and faculty development experience (2013–2025).

chapter 14

Curriculum Development — What Should We Teach and When?

"If you don't know where you are going, any road will take you there."
—Lewis Carroll

A bilingual program is more than books, schedules, or English class hours. It is a journey of growth, intentionality, and alignment. To build a successful bilingual school, you must decide **not only what content students will learn**, but **when and how** they will encounter it.

Curriculum development ensures that learning happens step by step, grade by grade, with intentional skill progression—not random disconnected lessons. When done well, the curriculum becomes a roadmap guiding students from their first English sounds in preschool to academic fluency, confidence, and certification readiness by graduation.

Why a Curriculum Roadmap Matters

Without a clear roadmap:

- Lesson planning becomes inconsistent
- Teachers repeat or skip skills
- Students develop gaps in grammar, fluency, or writing
- Assessment becomes unclear
- Parents and administrators lose confidence

A well-structured bilingual curriculum:

- Creates continuity
- Supports teacher growth
- Ensures alignment with standards
- Makes evaluation meaningful
- Protects the long-term vision

Three Anchors of a Strong Bilingual Curriculum

Your curriculum should be built on three interconnected components:

1. Language skill progression

Students need clear milestones in:

- Speaking
- Listening
- Reading
- Writing

- Academic vocabulary
- Fluency and pronunciation

Language learning is cumulative—each year should build upon the last.

2. Academic content integration

Your curriculum should identify:

- Which subjects can transition into English
- When the transition should begin
- How language support scaffolds content

For example:

Grade Level	% of Instruction in English	Focus
Preschool	Exposure only	Vocabulary + songs
Elementary	20-40%	Phonics + classroom language + basic content
Middle School	40-60%	Academic reading + writing + CLIL
High School	60%+	Certification readiness + literature + debate

3. Cultural and certification alignment

A bilingual program should prepare students for:

- National benchmarks
- International standards (CEFR, Common Core, Cambridge, IELTS, etc.)
- Cross-cultural competencies
- Future academic or professional pathways

Students should graduate not only bilingual, but also globally capable.

Building Your Curriculum: Step-by-Step

1. Start with your mission and vision.
Does your school aim for bilingual competency, biliteracy, biculturalism, or certification-level fluency?

2. Identify required standards.
Use CEFR, Common Core ESL frameworks, or country-specific guidelines mentions differentiation of language models relevant to planning.

3. Choose teaching approaches and methodology.
(Aligned with your earlier decisions in Chapters 3–5.)

4. Create grade-level targets.
Define yearly expectations in skill, vocabulary, fluency, reading, and academic writing.

5. Select or build instructional materials.
Remember: "The book is not the program."

6. Plan assessments.
Diagnostic, formative, and summative evaluation must match learning goals.

7. Review and improve annually.
Curriculum is not a museum artifact. It evolves.

A Simple Curriculum Planning Template

Category	Preschool	Primary	Middle	High School
Language Skills	Phonics, vocabulary	Foundational fluency	Academic language	Certification-level fluency

Category	Preschool	Primary	Middle	High School
Reading	Picture books	Graded readers	Novels + articles	Literature + research
Speaking	Songs + routines	Basic conversation	Debate + presentations	Rhetoric + academic argument
Writing	Tracing letters	Paragraphs	Essays	Research + exam writing
Cultural Focus	Holidays + songs	Geography + simple history	Literature + values	Global citizenship

A Biblical View of Planning

For faith-based institutions, curriculum development is also stewardship.

"Commit to the Lord whatever you do, and He will establish your plans."
—Proverbs 16:3

Excellence is not accidental—it is intentional and prayerful.

Reflection

What part of your current curriculum needs clarity—scope, sequence, standards, assessment, or alignment?

Write your next step, not your final answer.

References

Cambridge English Benchmarks.

CEFR Language Framework.

TESOL Scope and Sequence Models.

Author experience in program design (2015–2025).

chapter 15

Engaging Parents and the Community in Your Bilingual Program

"Education is a partnership. When the school, the family, and the community walk together, children flourish."—Unknown

A bilingual program is not built only by administrators, teachers, or curriculum. It requires cooperation from students, families, and the community. When parents understand the vision, support the goals, and participate in the learning journey, the bilingual program becomes stronger, more respected, and more sustainable.

However, when parents misunderstand the process—especially the time, patience, and consistency required for language development—unnecessary pressure can arise. Some parents may compare schools unfairly, expect instant fluency, or assume that purchasing a textbook automatically guarantees results.

For a bilingual program to thrive, families must feel informed, respected, and invited into the mission—not simply notified.

Why Parent Engagement Matters

Parents are critical allies in bilingual education because:

- They influence motivation at home
- They reinforce habits and routines
- They shape student attitudes toward effort and struggle
- They help maintain consistency when progress feels slow
- They advocate for the school within the community

A well-informed parent becomes an ambassador. A confused parent becomes a critic.

Avoiding Common Misunderstandings

In many bilingual schools, parents ask:

- *"Why isn't my child fluent yet?"*
- *"Why is the teacher speaking English if my child doesn't understand?"*
- *"Why is my child making mistakes in Spanish now?"*
- *"Why do we need grammar if they can already speak?"*

These questions are not signs of resistance—they are signs of curiosity and concern. Our role is to guide families through the process so they can support learning rather than fear it.

Communicating Clearly and Consistently

Your communication strategy should include:

Communication Type	Frequency	Purpose
Parent orientation sessions	Once per year	Explain expectations, vision, and methodology
Progress meetings	Once per term	Celebrate growth and clarify next goals
Workshops	1-3 times per year	Teach parents how to support learning at home
Written updates/newsletters	Monthly or bimonthly	Share milestones, events, and strategies
Open-house or classroom showcase	At least once annually	Allow students to demonstrate progress publicly

When communication is proactive, parents feel confident. When communication is reactive, parents become anxious.

Helping Parents Understand Language Growth

Parents need to understand that language learning develops in stages:

1. Silent/receptive phase
2. Early production
3. Structured speaking
4. Free communication
5. Academic fluency and literacy

If families expect stage five in the first year, frustration replaces joy. Remind them:

Progress is not always visible in the beginning—but it is always happening.

Creating a Culture of Celebration

A powerful way to engage families is through public celebration:

- English fairs
- Debate competitions
- Reading festivals
- Cultural immersion days
- Certification ceremonies
- Performances and exhibitions

Celebration makes learning visible and meaningful. Parents stop asking, *"Is this working?"* and begin saying, *"Look how far they have come!"*

Community Partnerships

Consider connecting your bilingual program to:

- Local universities
- International schools
- Embassy cultural centers
- Language institutes
- Mission organizations (for Christian schools)
- Study-abroad or exchange programs

When bilingualism becomes part of community identity, your school becomes a regional reference—not just another option.

A Spiritual Perspective

For Christian institutions, engaging families is also a ministry.

"Encourage one another and build each other up."—1 Thessalonians 5:11

We are not simply teaching English—we are building confidence, faith, and opportunity.

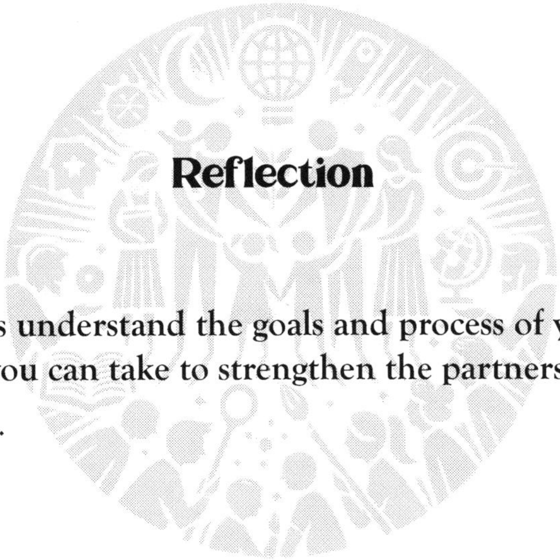

Reflection

How well do your parents understand the goals and process of your bilingual program—and what is one step you can take to strengthen the partnership?

Write it. Share it. Begin it.

References

Cambridge English Parental Support Toolkit.
TESOL Parent Engagement Framework.
Author field interviews with bilingual school communities (2014-2025).

chapter 16

Launching Your Bilingual Program — The First 90 Days

"Small steps done consistently create big change."—James Clear

Launching a bilingual program is an exciting moment for a school. It represents vision, courage, faith, and a commitment to preparing students for a global future. But enthusiasm alone is not enough. The first 90 days will determine whether your bilingual initiative begins with clarity and momentum—or confusion and hesitation.

This chapter provides a roadmap for the first three months so your school can begin with confidence, structure, and unity.

Before Day One: Prepare Your Foundations

A successful launch begins **before** students arrive.

1. Administrative priorities

- Confirm the program model and goals
- Communicate expectations to faculty
- Finalize curriculum alignment and schedules
- Prepare classrooms and bilingual routines
- Ensure technology, books, and resources are in place

2. Spiritual or mission alignment (if applicable)

Open your launch with prayer, purpose, and unity.

> *"Unless the Lord builds the house, the builders labor in vain."*
> —Psalm 127:1

This is not only a program—it is an investment in lives and futures.

3. Month 1: Building culture and consistency

The first month is about establishing patterns—not perfection. Focus on:

- Classroom English routines
- Teacher communication in English
- Clear lesson structures
- Introducing songs, vocabulary, and expectations
- Speaking opportunities every lesson

Parents, students, and teachers should feel:

- Excited
- Supported

- Clear about what is happening

Avoid overwhelming changes. Slow and steady builds confidence.

4. Month 2: Strengthening skills and processes

Once routines are established, deepen instruction. Focus on:

- Balanced use of listening, speaking, reading, and writing
- Visual supports, scaffolding, and modeling
- Beginning assessment to track early progress
- Teacher coaching and classroom observation
- Encouraging student participation and confidence

Continue parent communication—celebrate visible progress.

5. Month 3: Evaluating, adjusting, celebrating

The last month of the launch phase is about reflection and refinement, not judgment. Ask:

- What is working well?
- What needs adjustment?
- Where do teachers need support?
- What are parents noticing?
- What signs of growth do we see?

Celebrate breakthroughs—even small ones:

- A shy student speaking for the first time
- A class conducting morning routines fully in English
- A parent noticing more English at home

Celebration builds identity.

A Sample First 90-Day Action Plan

Week Range	Focus	Outcome
Weeks 1-2	Routines + consistency	Students recognize expectations
Weeks 3-4	Teacher collaboration + coaching	Faculty aligned and supported
Weeks 5-6	Skills development + curriculum pacing	Academic progress begins
Weeks 7-8	Parent reinforcement and workshops	Families engaged and informed
Weeks 9-12	Evaluation, reflection, and celebration	Confidence and momentum established

Leadership Mindset: Calm, Clear, Consistent

During the launch, leaders must:

- Communicate clearly
- Support teachers
- Protect the mission from pressure or panic
- Celebrate consistency over speed
- Model patience and long-term thinking

Remember: bilingual education is a marathon—not a sprint.

A Word of Encouragement

Language growth often feels invisible at first, like seeds planted under soil. But over time, confidence grows, vocabulary expands, and English becomes part of school identity.

"Do not despise these small beginnings, for the Lord rejoices to see the work begin."
—Zechariah 4:10 (NLT)

The first 90 days are not about perfection—but direction.

Reflection Question

What will be your first visible action to launch your bilingual program with clarity and momentum?

Write it down. Share it. Then do it.

References

TESOL International: Program Startup Guidelines
Cambridge School Launch Framework
Author experience consulting bilingual school launches (2015–2025)

chapter 17

Be Patient — Bilingualism Takes Time

"The day you plant the seed is not the day you eat the fruit."
—African Proverb

One of the greatest challenges in bilingual education is patience—not only from students, but from teachers, parents, and school leaders. Language development is a slow, layered, and sometimes invisible journey. Progress is happening, but not always in a way that can be immediately measured.

Many schools underestimate the emotional side of bilingual learning. Students may feel frustrated when words don't come out fluently. Teachers may feel discouraged when students struggle. Parents may worry when results are not instant. Administrators may fear the community's expectations.

In these moments, it is essential to remember:

Bilingual education is not fast—it is transformational.

Understanding the Timeline of Language Growth

Language acquisition follows natural stages. Every learner moves through them:

1. Exposure and Listening
The brain absorbs sounds even before producing language.

2. Emerging Production
Short phrases, repetition, imitation.

3. Structured Speech
Sentences with predictable patterns.

4. Free Expression
Confidence to speak in unfamiliar situations.

5. Academic Language and Literacy
The ability to analyze, debate, write, and think in English.

It may take months for visible progress—and **years** before mastery. And that is normal.

The Silent Phase Is Still Progress

Some students will speak early. Others will listen quietly for weeks—sometimes months. Silence is not failure. Silence is processing. Just as a child listens before speaking their first language, students learning a second language build understanding before vocabulary. The quiet stage is not empty—it is **foundational.**

The Silent Phase Is Still Progress

A rushed bilingual program creates anxiety. A consistent bilingual program creates confidence.

When teachers:

- Use English regularly
- Maintain routines
- Offer gentle correction
- Celebrate attempts

students begin to feel safe enough to try. And trying is where learning begins.

Avoiding the Pressure Trap

Pressure does not accelerate bilingualism—it restricts it. Avoid phrases like:

- "You should be fluent by now."
- "Why can't you say it correctly?"
- "Your classmates know this already."

Instead say:

✔ *"You're learning–keep going."*

✔ *"That was a great effort."*

✔ *"Try again–you're improving."*

Language grows in environments where students feel **brave, not afraid.**

Measuring Progress Wisely

True bilingual progress is seen in:

- Increased confidence
- More attempts
- Greater comprehension
- Longer responses

- Improved pronunciation
- Growing vocabulary
- Willingness to speak without being asked

These milestones are more meaningful than a test score.

Supporting Teachers Through the Long Journey

Teachers also need encouragement. They may wonder:

- *"Am I doing enough?"*
- *"Are my students learning?"*
- *"Why is this slower than expected?"*

Create a culture where teachers hear:

✔ "Thank you for your consistency."
✔ "Your work matters."
✔ "You are shaping something permanent."

Teachers who feel valued stay committed—and committed teachers make bilingual programs succeed.

Encouraging Parents to Trust the Process

Parents often want results as fast as possible. It helps to remind them:

- Language growth happens with repetition
- Mistakes are part of learning
- Fluency comes with time and confidence
- Improvement can look invisible before it becomes obvious

Parents are partners—guide them lovingly.

A Spiritual Perspective on Waiting

For Christian schools, patience is not just a strategy—it is a spiritual discipline.

"Do not grow weary in doing good, for at the proper time we will reap a harvest if we do not give up."—Galatians 6:9

Language learning is sowing, watering, waiting—and eventually harvesting. Your role is faithfulness.

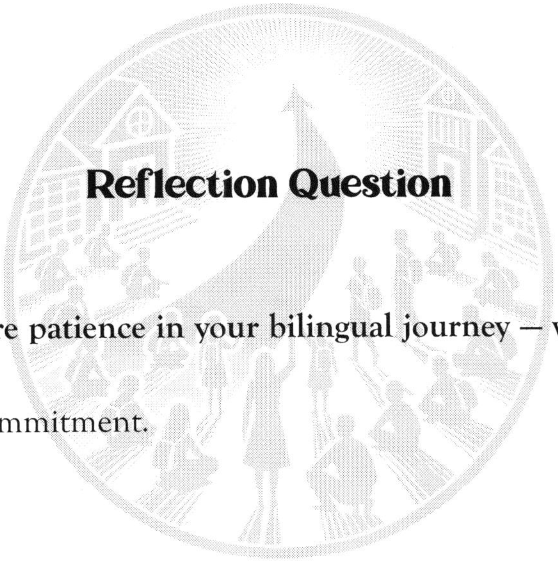

Reflection Question

Where do you need more patience in your bilingual journey — with students, teachers, parents, or yourself?

Write one sentence of commitment.

References

Cummins, J. (1981). *The Linguistic Interdependence Hypothesis.*

Krashen, S. (1982). *Principles and Practice in Second Language Acquisition.*

Author classroom observations and bilingual leadership experiences (2014–2025).

chapter 18

Moving Forward With Purpose — Your Bilingual Journey Begins

"The future belongs to those who prepare for it today."
—Malcolm X

You have walked through the vision, strategy, tools, mindset, and structure required to build a bilingual school. You have explored curriculum, methodology, evaluation, faculty development, parent engagement, and the patience needed for growth. Now, you stand at the beginning of a journey that will bless generations.

Building a bilingual program is not about achieving perfection—it is about committing to purpose. Every step—even the imperfect ones—moves your school closer to transformation.

This chapter offers two final gifts:

clarity for the path ahead, and encouragement to continue with confidence.

A Final Roadmap: What Happens Next

You don't need to do everything at once. Instead, move forward intentionally. Here is a suggested 12-24 month progression:

Phase 1 — Establish the Foundation (Months 1-6)

- Confirm the bilingual model
- Train teachers in methodology and routines
- Implement classroom English practices
- Communicate clearly with parents
- Begin small assessment methods

Goal: Culture and consistency before complexity.

Phase 2 — Grow Instructional Strength (Months 6-12)

- Expand language objectives
- Add reading and writing routines
- Strengthen lesson planning alignment
- Support teachers with coaching and collaboration
- Continue communicating progress

Goal: Visible improvement in language confidence.

Phase 3 — Deepen Academic Integration (Year 2)

- Introduce CLIL subjects (science, history, art, etc.)
- Prepare students for international benchmarks
- Strengthen bilingual leadership structure
- Celebrate learning publicly

Goal: English becomes part of the identity of the school – not only part of the schedule.

A Checklist for Ongoing Success

Use this annually to realign your program:

Question	Yes	Needs Work
Do teachers consistently use English during instruction?	☐	☐
Does the curriculum align with long-term goals?	☐	☐
Are parents informed and engaged?	☐	☐
Is teacher training ongoing and purposeful?	☐	☐
Is progress being measured and reviewed regularly?	☐	☐
Is the program improving year after year?	☐	☐

This checklist is not a test. It is a compass.

A Word to Leaders

You will face questions. You will face pressure. You will face moments where you wonder if the effort is worth it. During those moments, return to your *why*:

- Students deserve access to opportunity.
- Students deserve a voice beyond borders.
- Students deserve the confidence that comes from bilingual identity.

Your leadership will open doors they cannot yet see.

A Word to Teachers

Your work matters more than you know. Some days you may feel unseen, unheard, or exhausted. But every flashcard, every phrase, every moment of patience, every attempt to encourage — they are seeds planted in hearts and minds.

You are helping students believe: *"I can learn. I can speak. I can belong anywhere in the world."* That is a gift few professions can claim.

A Word to Parents

Thank you for trusting the process, for encouraging your children, and for believing in their potential. Your patience, support, and consistency make the difference.

Bilingualism is not just a skill—it is an inheritance.

A Word to Students

Be brave. There will be days that English feels hard. Days when mistakes feel embarrassing. Days when speaking requires courage.

But remember—every great skill begins with trying. And every time you try, you get better.

A Spiritual Blessing (For Faith-Based Schools)

If your school is rooted in faith, then remember:

> *"I can do all things through Christ who gives me strength."*—Philippians 4:13

God equips those He calls—and He has called you to this work.

Your Calling Moves Forward

This book is not the end—it is the beginning. Your bilingual program will grow step by step, year by year, through:

- Excellence
- Unity
- Patience
- Faith
- Commitment

And one day, you will look at a graduating class speaking confidently in two languages and realize:

🗨 *"This was worth everything."*

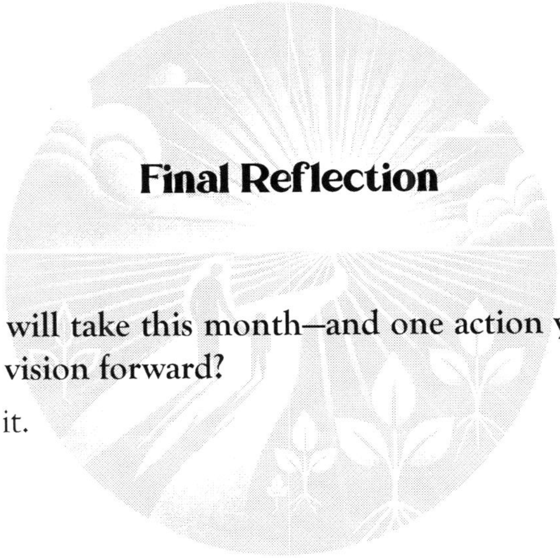

Final Reflection

What is one action you will take this month—and one action you will take this year—to move your bilingual vision forward?

Write it. Share it. Begin it.

Conclusion

The journey to bilingual education is long, meaningful, and transformational. You are now equipped, prepared, and empowered. You have a roadmap — and you have a calling.

So go—lead boldly.

Your students are waiting.

Contact Yair at:
yairrhf@gmail.com